Strange ... E

WEREWOLVES

XINA M. UHL

BLACK
RABBIT
BOOKS

Bolt is published by Black Rabbit Books
P.O. Box 3263, Mankato, Minnesota, 56002.
www.blackrabbitbooks.com
Copyright © 2018 Black Rabbit Books

Marysa Storm, editor; Grant Gould, interior
designer; Michael Sellner, cover designer;
Omay Ayres, photo researcher

Library of Congress Cataloging-in-Publication Data
Names: Uhl, Xina M., author.
Title: Werewolves / by Xina M. Uhl.
Description: Mankato, Minnesota : Black Rabbit Books, [2018] | Series: Bolt.
Strange . . . but true? | Includes bibliographical references and index. |
Audience: Age 9-12. | Audience: Grade 4 to 6.
Identifiers: LCCN 2016049990 (print) | LCCN 2016058516 (ebook) | ISBN
9781680721850 (library binding) | ISBN 9781680722499 (e-book) | ISBN
9781680724820 (paperback)
Subjects: LCSH: Werewolves–Juvenile literature.
Classification: LCC GR830.W4 U36 2018 (print) | LCC GR830.W4 (ebook) |
DDC 398.24/54–dc23
LC record available at https://lccn.loc.gov/2016049990

Printed in the United States at CG Book Printers,
North Mankato, Minnesota, 56003. 3/17

Contents

CHAPTER 1

Howls and Haunts

In 1992, Tammy Bray drove home to her house in Wisconsin. Suddenly, she saw a large creature in front of her car. She slammed on the brakes. The creature had a doglike face and yellow eyes. It was covered in fur. Her husband had seen something similar earlier. Was it the same beast? Was it the Wisconsin Werewolf?

5

Some people think full moons bring trouble.
Some police officers agree. They say they're busier
during full moons. Some **emergency** medical workers
say full moon nights are crazier too.

The Curse

Sightings like Bray's aren't unheard of. And stories about werewolves have been around for hundreds of years.

Most werewolf stories talk about the full moon. They say it brings a **curse**. In the dark of night, some people change. They grow fangs. Fur covers their bodies. They growl and howl. They **crave** fresh meat. Are the stories **myths**? Or are the creatures real?

WEREWOLF FEATURES

FANGS

GOOD HEARING

FUR

CLAWS

CAN RUN LIKE A WOLF

CHAPTER 2

Spooky Stories

Tales about werewolves go back to **ancient** times. During the **Middle Ages**, people thought witches turned people into werewolves.

Stories about people changing into animals are told around the world. Wolves don't live everywhere. In places without wolves, stories say people turn into other animals.

What Else Do Humans Turn Into?

BEAR
(RUSSIAN AND NATIVE AMERICAN MYTHOLOGY)

TIGER
(ASIAN MYTHOLOGY)

• **LION**
(AFRICAN MYTHOLOGY)

Terrifying Tales

There are different ways someone can become a werewolf. Some stories say people are cursed. Others are born werewolves. Most stories say someone bitten by a werewolf will turn into one.

Most stories say a full moon **triggers** the **transformation**. The cursed cannot control the change. They can't fight the need to hunt. Other stories say some people have powers. They can turn into wolves when they want.

A plant called wolfsbane is deadly to humans. In many stories, it hurts werewolves too.

Monster Movies

Many of today's werewolf beliefs come from pop culture. Werewolves are common in books. They appear in many movies and TV shows too.

A movie called *The Wolf Man* came out in 1941. It and other movies tell similar stories. They are about people who are bitten by werewolves.

Many stories say silver hurts werewolves. *The Wolf Man* was one of the first movies to show this.

CHAPTER 3

Werewolf!

Werewolf stories in movies and books are made-up. But what about the stories and sightings from real life?

In 1589, a German farmer said he killed and ate many people. The story says he sold his soul to the devil. In return, the farmer could turn into a wolf.

From 1764 to 1767, a beast ran wild in France. It killed more than 100 people. Stories say a hunter used a silver bullet to kill the beast.

A WORLD OF WEREWOLVES

Werewolves could be all over the world. Attacks and sightings have been reported in many places.

UNITED KINGDOM

CANADA

UNITED STATES

HAITI

MEXICO

BRAZIL

GERMANY

RUSSIA

FRANCE

On the Prowl

There have been recent sightings too. People, like Bray, say there's a beast in Wisconsin. Nine people saw it from 1936 to 1999. They say it stands around 7 feet (2.1 meters) tall. It has pointed ears and yellow eyes.

There have been sightings in Hull, England, as well. Most sightings have been in a cemetery. Some people have reported seeing something huge and hairy. Others said they've heard howling.

OSTRICH

9 FEET (2.7 M)

WISCONSIN WEREWOLF

7 FEET (2.1 M)

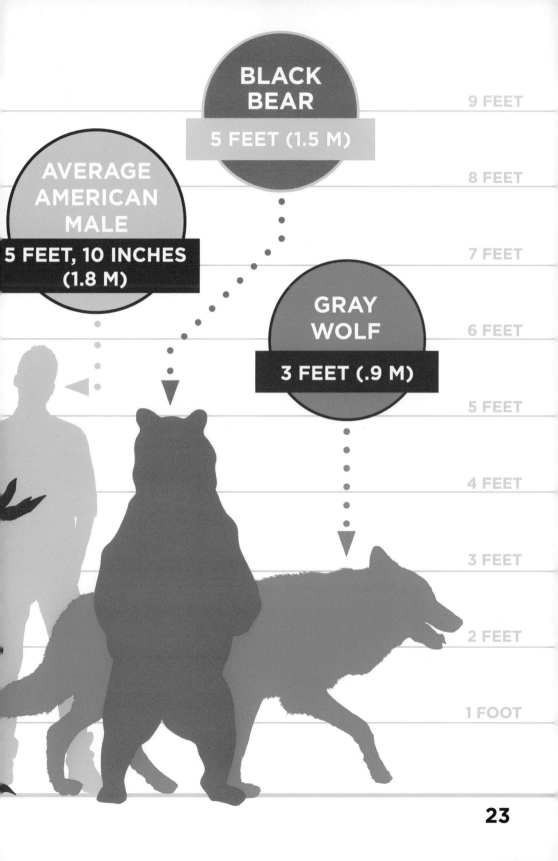

BLACK
BEAR

5 FEET (1.5 M)

AVERAGE
AMERICAN
MALE

5 FEET, 10 INCHES
(1.8 M)

GRAY
WOLF

3 FEET (.9 M)

9 FEET

8 FEET

7 FEET

6 FEET

5 FEET

4 FEET

3 FEET

2 FEET

1 FOOT

Werewolf Diseases

Hypertrichosis
Patches of hair cover a person's body.

Lycanthropy
A person believes he or she is an animal.

Porphyria
A person avoids light and has seizures and increased hair growth.

CHAPTER 4

Walking

Many people believe all werewolf stories are myths. They think science has the answers. An illness can cause people to grow thick patches of hair. The hair covers their bodies. It can make humans look like wolves.

A person's mind can get sick too. One disease makes people believe they aren't human. Instead, the people think they are animals. Did the German farmer have this disease?

Still a Mystery

Long ago, dark forests hid hungry wolves. People told stories about them. The stories said wolves had powers. Some believe werewolves came from these myths. Others think illnesses can explain werewolf stories.

But some people are not so sure. Today, people have a better understanding of illnesses. Werewolf sightings still occur, though. What do you think is happening?

Believe It or Not?

Answer the questions below. Then add up your points to see if you believe.

1 You see something furry running in the night. What is it?

A. It's a werewolf! (3 points)

B. I don't know. (2 points)

C. It's just a big dog. (1 point)

2 It's a full moon! What do you do?

A. Stay inside! (3 points)

B. Admire it. (2 points)

C. Nothing. It's just the moon. (1 point)

3 Reread page 17. What do you think about the German farmer?

A. He was totally a werewolf! (3 points)

B. I'd like to know more. (2 points)

C. He was probably ill. (1 point)

. . . .

3 points
There's no way the creatures are real.

4–8 points
Maybe they're real. But then again, maybe they're not.

9 points
You're a total believer!

29

ancient (AYN-shunt)—from a long time ago

crave (KREYV)—to want greatly

curse (KURS)—the cause of trouble or bad luck

emergency (ih-MUR-juhn-see)—something unexpected that requires immediate action

Middle Ages (MIH-duhl AY-juz)—having to do with the period of history between the 400s and 1400s

myth (MITH)—a story that was told in an ancient culture to explain a practice, belief, or natural occurrence

transformation (trans-fer-MEY-shun)—a change

trigger (TRIG-er)—something that causes something else to happen

BOOKS

Frisch, Aaron. *Werewolves.* That's Spooky! Mankato, MN: Creative Paperbacks, 2014.

Owen, Ruth. *Werewolves and Other Shape-Shifters.* Not Near Normal: The Paranormal. New York: Bearport Publishing, 2013.

Terp, Gail. *Gray Wolves.* Wild Animal Kingdom. Mankato, MN: Black Rabbit Books, 2017.

WEBSITES

Gray Wolf
kids.nationalgeographic.com/animals/gray-wolf/#gray-wolf-closeup.jpg

The Legend of Werewolves
www.kidzworld.com/article/24871-the-legend-of-werewolves

Monster 101: All About Werewolves
www.cbc.ca/kidscbc2/the-feed/monsters-101-all-about-werewolves

INDEX